To Aidan, my little brother.
May you never lose your love for cars and all things good.

Aidan was watching TV one day when he saw the coolest thing ever...

It was Aidan's favorite toy: race cars! The car was red with grey wheels and orange stripes.

Okie Dokie

Hey Aidan, it's time to go to the grocery store!

I think that's everything. Oh! What is it Aidan?

It's... THE NEWEST RACE CAR!

Mom! Mom! I want it!
Can we buy it?

Hmm... I have an idea. Why don't you open up a lemonade stand to earn the money for the car?

How To Run A Lemonade Stand!

STEPS

#1: Collect all the ingredients to make the lemonade (make sure to calculate the total cost of all the ingredients)

#2: Make the lemonade! (Page 24)

#3: Determine how much to sell the lemonade for (based on the ingredient costs + goals)

#4: Build a lemonade stand and find the best spot with the help of an adult

#5: Start selling lemonade!

#6: Clean up after

Water

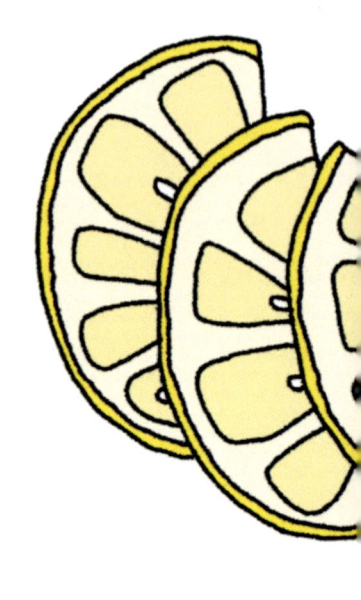

Ingredients

Lemons

Sugar

Cups and Straws

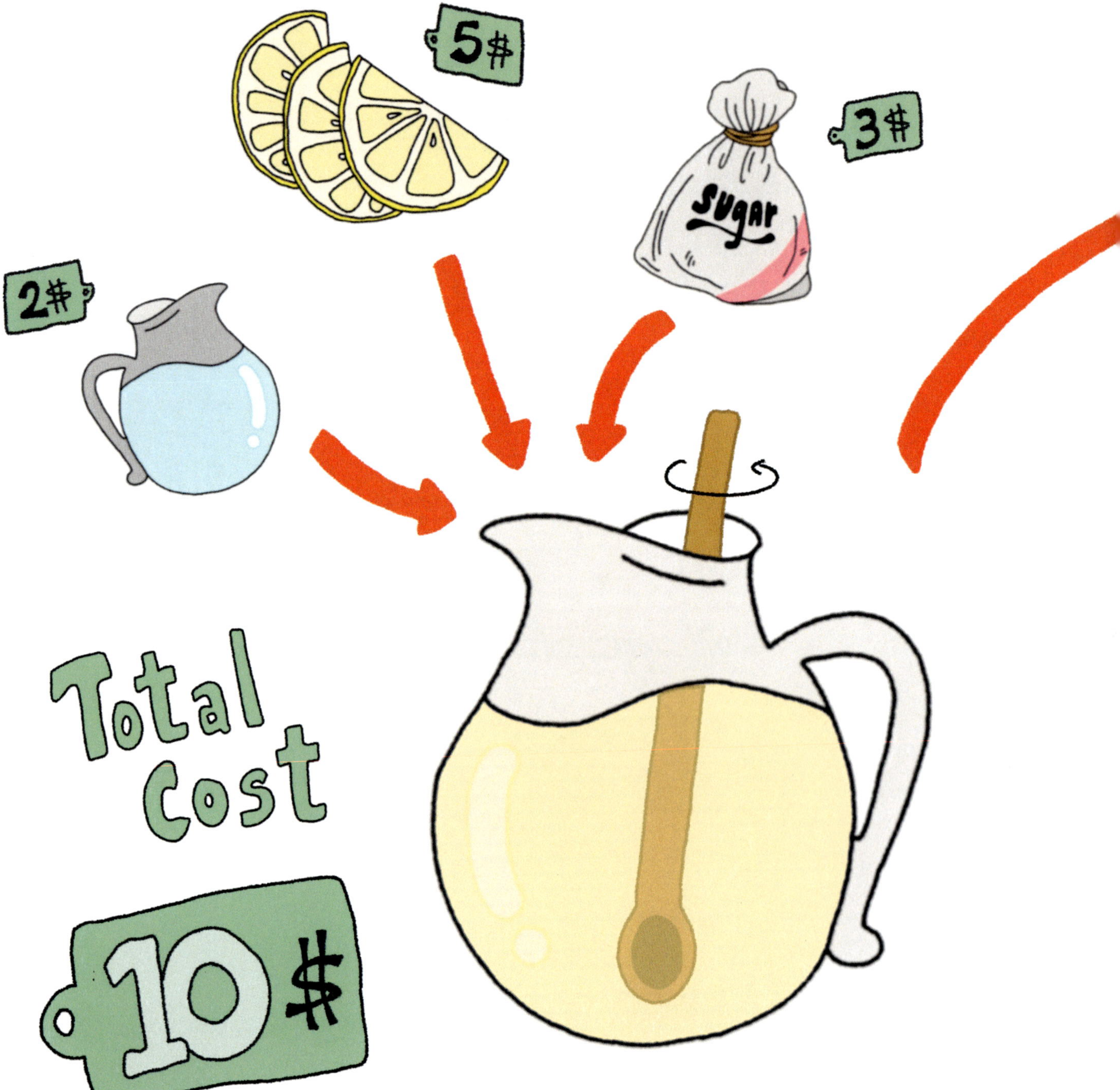
5$
3$
Sugar
2$
Total
Cost
10$

For 10 cups of lemonade!

$20 ÷ 10 cups = $2

How much should we sell the lemonade for?

$40 + $20 = 60

price of the race car — ingredient cost — how much we need to make

60 ÷ 10 cups = 6

We will sell each cup of lemonade for **6 dollars!**

We need to make 40 dollars in **net profit** to get the race car! To do that, we need to make 60 dollars in **revenue** to make up for our ingredient costs.

$40 → NET PROFIT

Net Profit: the money we make from selling the lemonades minus the cost of the ingredients

60 → REVENUE

Revenue: the money we make from selling the lemonades

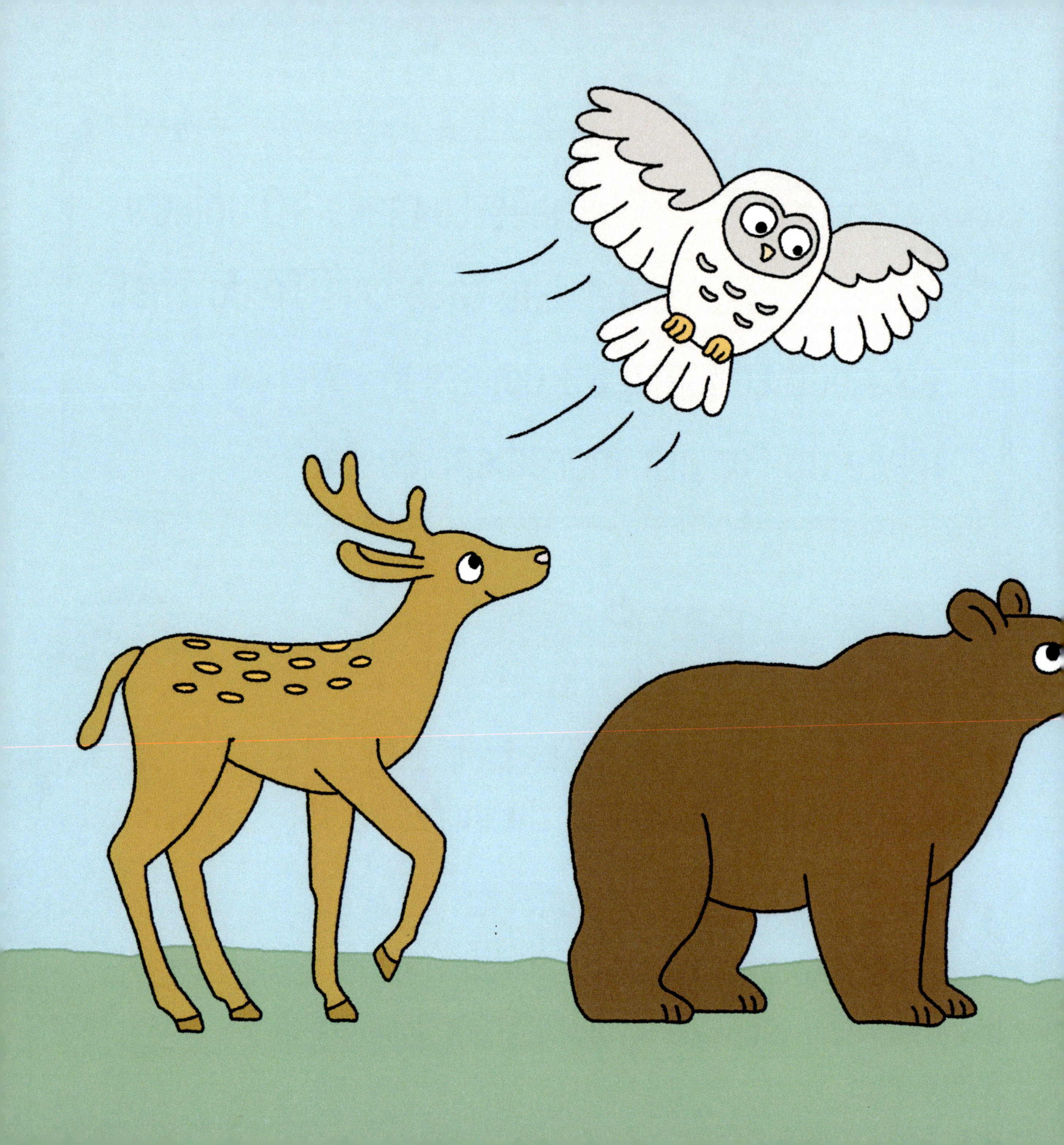

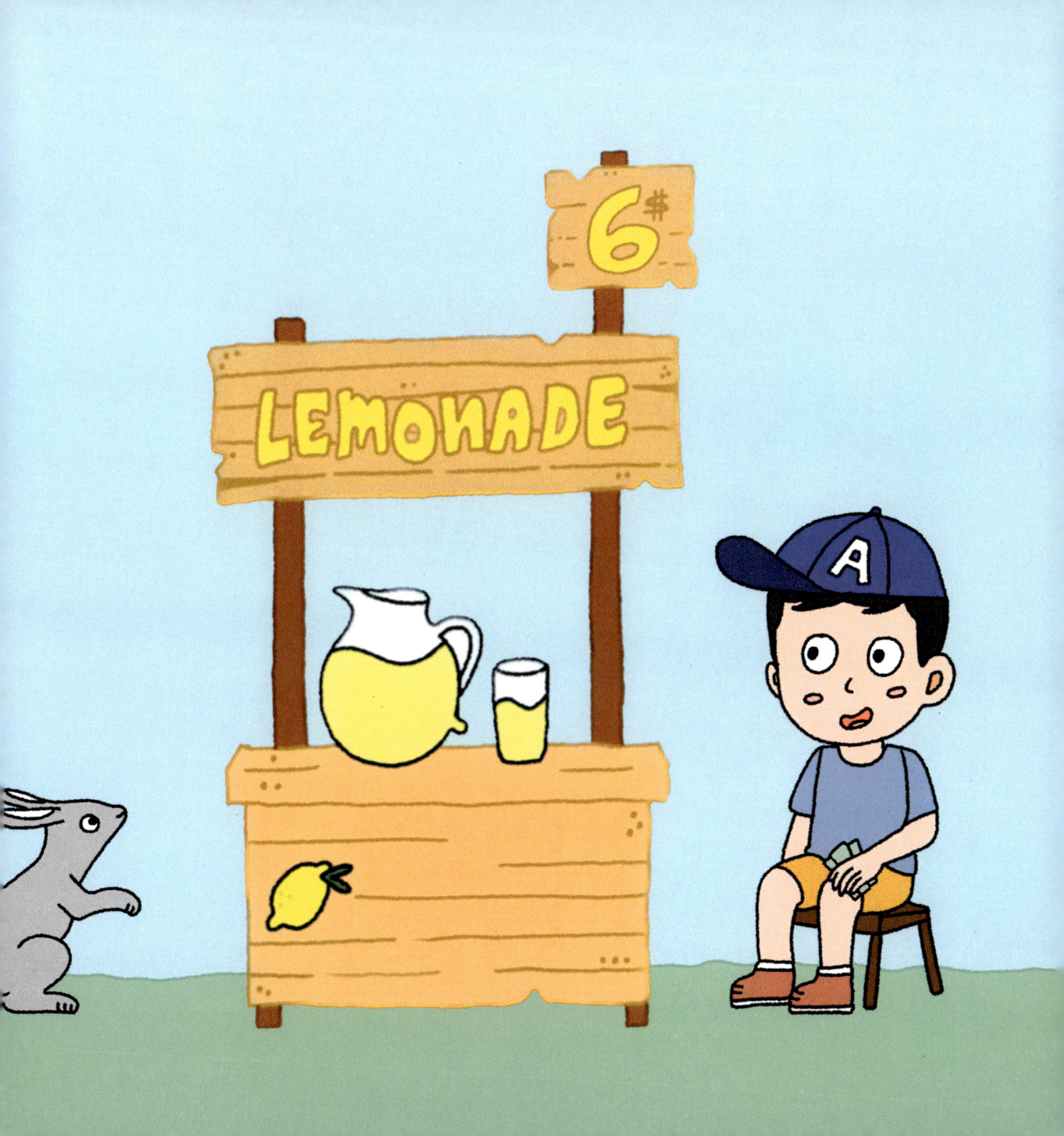
6$
LEMONADE
A

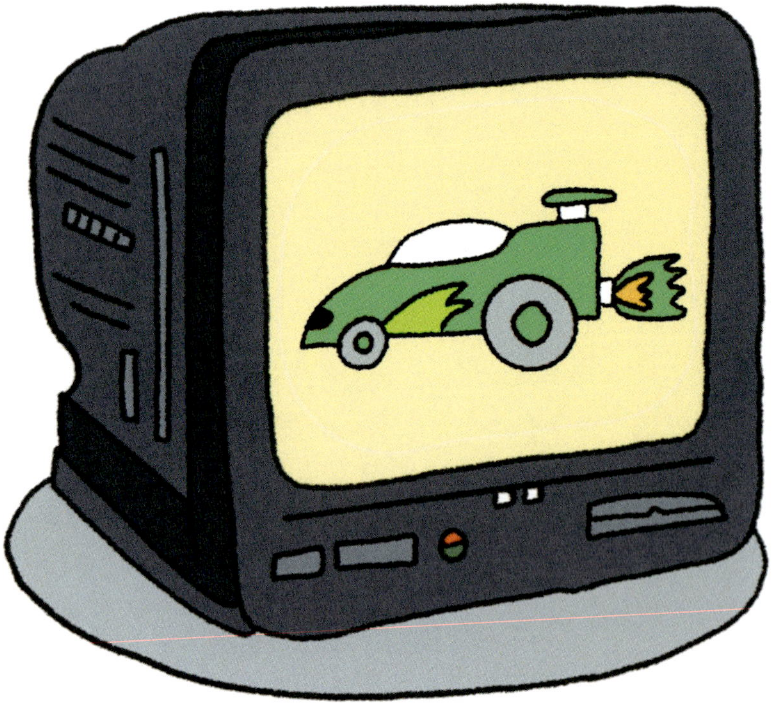

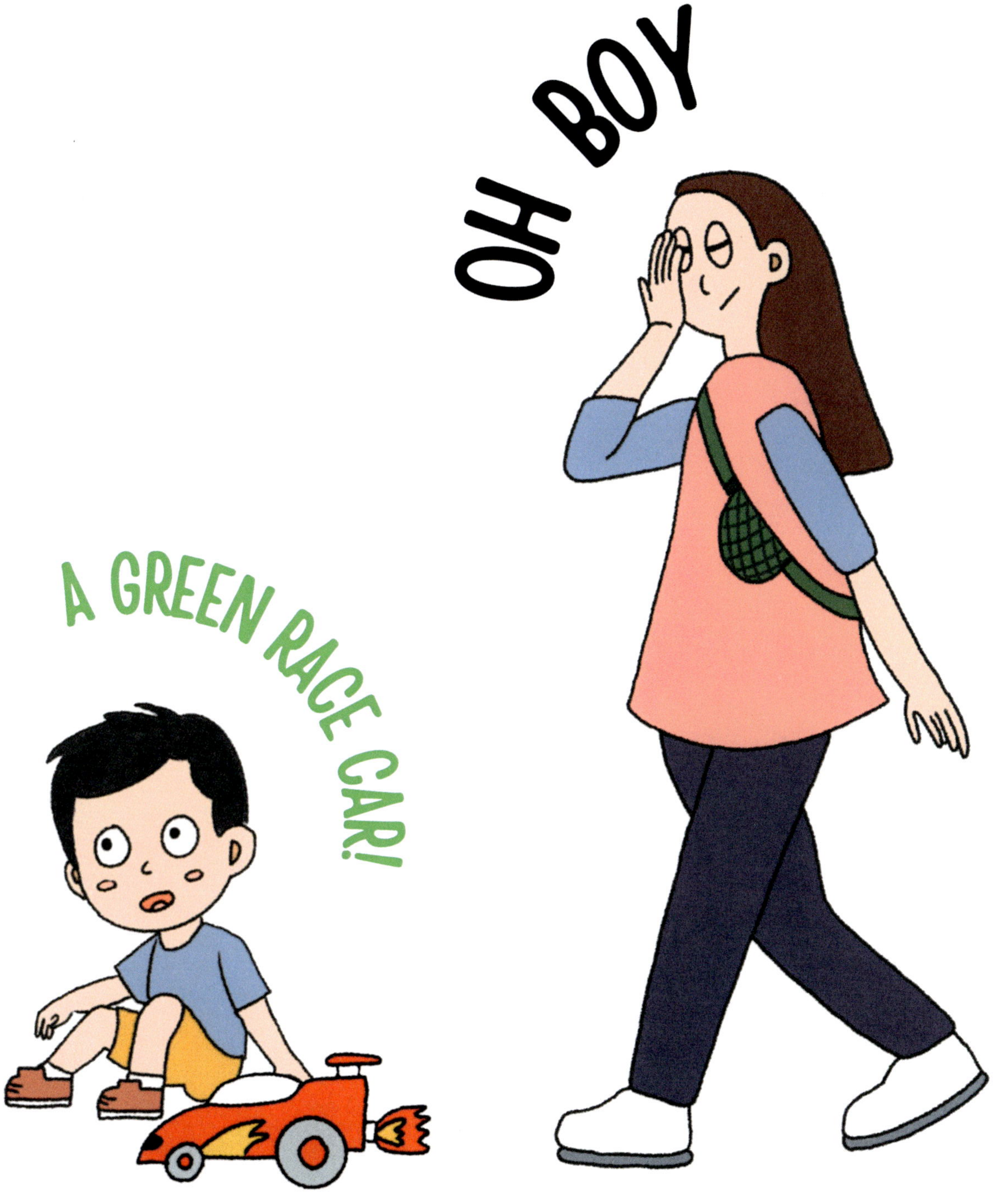
OH BOY
A GREEN RACE CAR!

Bonus Activity!
Can you match the cars by color?

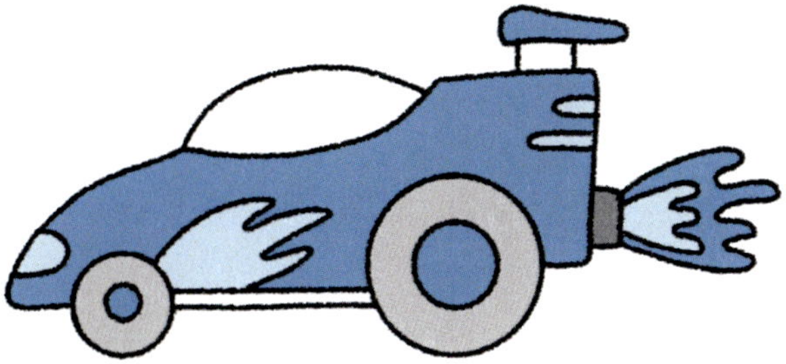
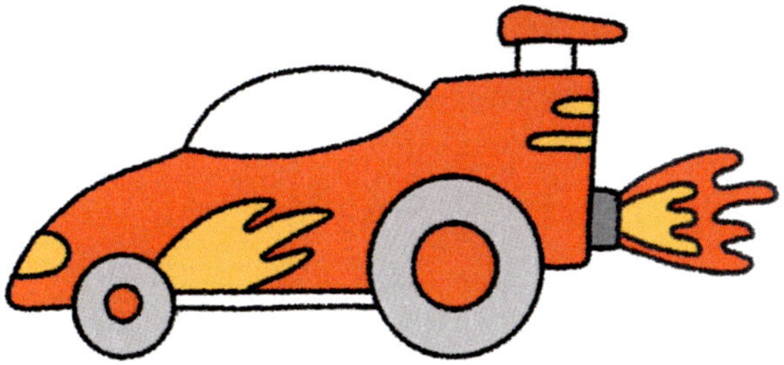
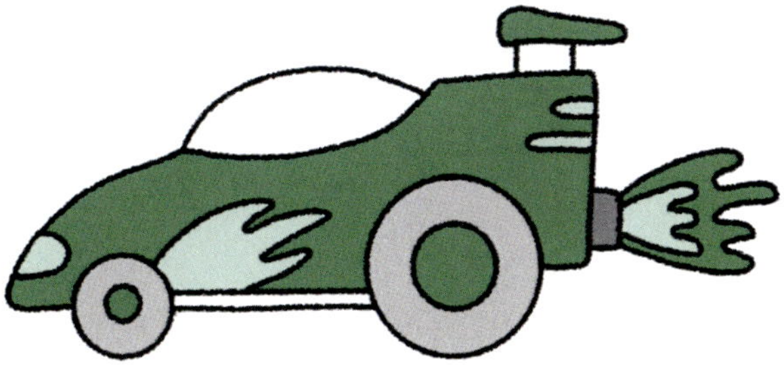
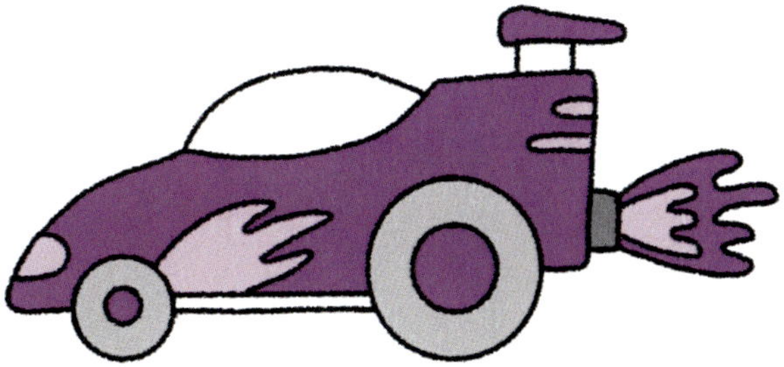
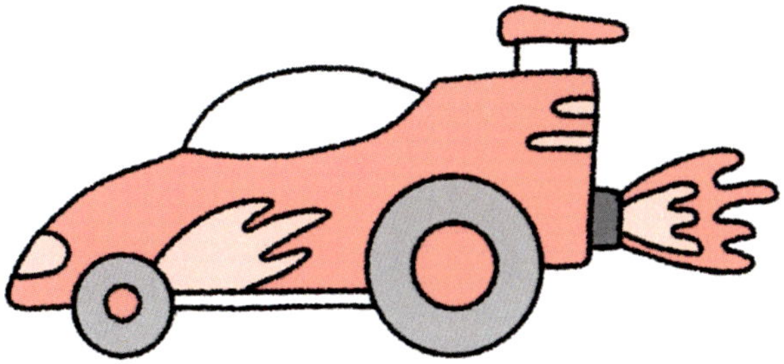
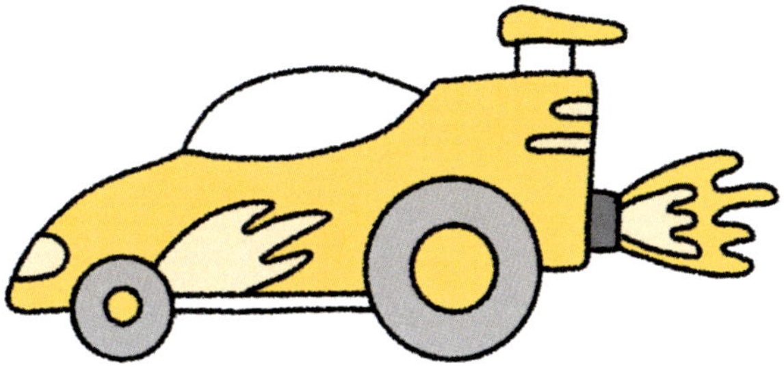
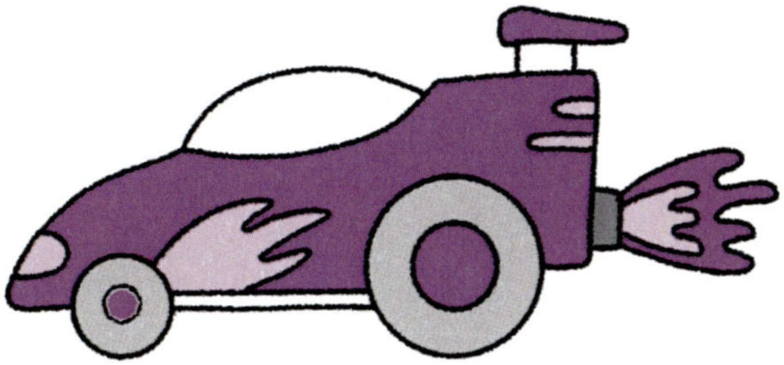
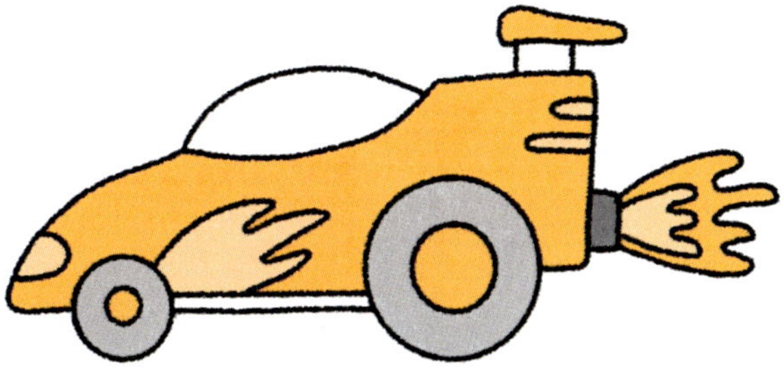

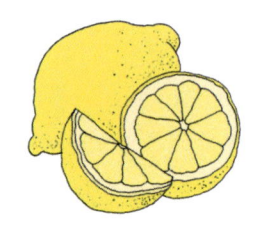

The Best Lemonade Recipe

1 cup of freshly squeezed lemon juice

3 cups of water

1 cup of sugar

Ice and lemon slices for garnish

Combine the lemon juice, water, and sugar together until the sugar is dissolved.

Add ice and lemon slices for garnish.

Enjoy!

Made in the USA
Las Vegas, NV
11 May 2025